First World War
and Army of Occupation
War Diary
France, Belgium and Germany

48 DIVISION
Divisional Troops
B Squadron King Edward's Horse
21 April 1915 - 31 May 1916

WO95/2749/1

The Naval & Military Press Ltd
www.nmarchive.com

Published in association with The National Archives

Published by

The Naval & Military Press Ltd

Unit 10 Ridgewood Industrial Park,

Uckfield, East Sussex,

TN22 5QE England

Tel: +44 (0) 1825 749494

www.naval-military-press.com

www.nmarchive.com

This diary has been reprinted in facsimile from the original. Any imperfections are inevitably reproduced and the quality may fall short of modern type and cartographic standards.

© Crown Copyright
Images reproduced by permission of The National Archives, London, England, 2015.

Contents

Document type	Place/Title	Date From	Date To
Heading	WO95/2749/1 B Squadron King Edward's Horse April 1915-May 1916		
Heading	48th Division 'B' Sqdn King Edward's Horse Apr 1915-May 1916		
Heading	48th Division "B" Squad King Edwards Horse (Divl Coy 49th Division) Vol I		
Heading	War Diary Of "B" Squadron King Edwards Horse From 21st April 1915 To 31st July 1915 Volume I		
War Diary		21/04/1915	21/04/1915
War Diary	Havre	22/04/1915	23/04/1915
War Diary	Nieppe	24/04/1915	26/06/1915
War Diary	Vieux Berquin	27/06/1915	27/06/1915
War Diary	Busnes	28/06/1915	28/06/1915
War Diary	Burbure	29/06/1915	30/06/1915
War Diary	Vieux Berquin	27/06/1915	27/06/1915
War Diary	Busnes	28/06/1915	28/06/1915
War Diary	Burbure	29/06/1915	19/07/1915
War Diary	Thievres	20/07/1915	21/07/1915
War Diary	Authie	22/07/1915	31/07/1915
Heading	48th Division B Squad King Edwards Horse (48th Divl Cavalry) Vol II Aug Sept 15		
Heading	War Diary Of B Squadron King Edwards Horse From 1.8.15 To 30.IX.15 (Volume I)		
War Diary	Bus Les Artois	01/08/1915	30/09/1915
Heading	48th Divn B Squadron King Edwards Horse (48th Divl Coy) Vol III Oct 15		
Heading	War Diary Of B Squadron King Edwards Horse (K.O.D.R) From 1st Oct 1915 To 31st Oct 1915 (Volume I)		
War Diary	Bus	01/10/1915	23/10/1915
War Diary	Bus Les Artois	24/10/1915	31/10/1915
Heading	48th Division War Diary Of B Squadron King Edwards Horse From 1st Nov 1915 To 30th Nov 1915 (Volume IV)		
War Diary	Bus	01/11/1915	27/11/1915
War Diary	Bus Les Artois	28/11/1915	30/11/1915
Heading	War Diary Of B Squadron King Edwards Horse K.O.D.R. From December 1st To 31st 1915 Vol V		
War Diary	Bus Les Artois	01/12/1915	31/12/1915
Heading	War Diary Of B Squadron King Edwards Horse (K.O.D.R.) From Jan 1st-31st 1916 Vol VI		
War Diary	Bus Les Artois	01/01/1916	27/01/1916
War Diary	Bus	27/01/1916	31/01/1916
Heading	War Diary Of "B" Squadron King Edwards Horse K.O.D.R. From Feb 1st-Feb 29th 1916 Vol VII		
War Diary	Bus Les Artois	01/02/1916	29/02/1916
Heading	War Diary Of "B" Sqdn King Edwards Horse From 1st March To 31st Mar 1916 Vol VIII		
War Diary	Bus Les Artois	01/03/1916	25/03/1916
War Diary	Couin	26/03/1916	31/03/1916

Heading	War Diary Of "B" Sqdn King Edwards Horse K.O.D.R From April 1st To 30th 1916 Vol IX		
War Diary	Couin	01/04/1916	11/04/1916
War Diary	St Ouen	12/04/1916	12/04/1916
War Diary	Acheux-En-Vimeu	13/04/1916	20/04/1916
War Diary	St Riquier	21/04/1916	25/04/1916
War Diary	St Ouen	26/04/1916	26/04/1916
War Diary	Couin	27/04/1916	30/04/1916
Heading	War Diary Of "B" Sqdn King Edwards Horse From 1st May 1916-May 31st 1916		
War Diary	Couin	01/05/1916	09/05/1916
War Diary	Ecoivres	10/05/1916	11/05/1916
War Diary	Chocques	11/05/1916	12/05/1916
War Diary	Marest	13/05/1916	16/05/1916
War Diary	Valhuon	17/05/1916	31/05/1916
Miscellaneous	O.C. B Sqdn 1st King Edwards Horse	02/06/1916	02/06/1916

WO 95/2749/1
11/6th L/5 O M
B Squadron King Edward's Horse
April 1915 — May 1916

48TH DIVISION   BEF

'B' SQDN KING EDWARD'S HORSE
APR 1915-MAY 1916

To
IV CORPS 1916 JUNE

48th Division

121/6357

"B" Squadⁿ King Edward's Horse
(Div^l Cav 48th Division)

Vol I

21-4 — 31-7-15

Apr '15
May '15

Confidential

War Diary of
'B' Squadron King Edwards Horse
from 21st April 1915 to 31st July 1915

Volume I

Army Form C. 2118.

WAR DIARY of 'B' Squadron. P. 1
or
INTELLIGENCE SUMMARY. King Edward Horse.

(Erase heading not required.)

Instructions regarding War Diaries and Intelligence Summaries are contained in F. S. Regs., Part II and the Staff Manual respectively. Title pages will be prepared in manuscript.

Place	Date	Hour	Summary of Events and Information	Remarks and references to Appendices
	Apr 21st		B. Sqdn KING EDWARD'S HORSE entrained at BISHOPS STORTFORD during night April 20-21st for service with the Expeditionary Force. 1st ½ Sqdn under Capt FURSE left at 3.30 am Wed Apr 21st; remainder at 5.30 am under Major M.F. DICK — 1st ½ Sqdn arrived SOUTHAMPTON at 8.45 am and embarked at once on S.S. PALM BRANCH, followed by 2nd train at 11.30 am 'C' Sqdn arrived & embarked during afternoon and ship sailed at 5.30 pm. The shackles on upper deck near Engine room were unhealthily set, there being no temp draft in on stable. RAF	
HAVRE	Apr 22nd	3 am	Ship arrived at HAVRE about 3 am. Disembarkation began 7 am and was carried out very smoothly — Both Squadrons marched to No 6 BASE CAMP. 1 horse was cast to about kick. This was the only casualty on the journey. RAF	
HAVRE	Apr 23		Three horses were cast (1 skin trouble – 2 kicks) and replaced by	

Army Form C. 2118.

WAR DIARY
or
INTELLIGENCE SUMMARY.
(Erase heading not required.)

Instructions regarding War Diaries and Intelligence Summaries are contained in F. S. Regs., Part II. and the Staff Manual respectively. Title pages will be prepared in manuscript.

Place	Date	Hour	Summary of Events and Information	Remarks and references to Appendices
HAVRE	Ap 22 (sat)	4pm	Interior train from Remount Depot. Marched to GARE AES MARCHANDISES 4pm - entraining on our train and left at 8pm.	
		8pm		
NIEPPE	Ap 24.	7.45pm	Arrived STEENWERCK STN 7.45 pm and detrained; marched (3½ miles) to billets at farm (3½ miles) on NIEPPE — LES TROIS TILLEULS road — and went into billets — Map 20.000 The whole journey from ENGLAND including en-and de-training, embarkation etc was satisfactory and was carried out more smoothly and quickly than was expected from inexperienced troops. There was only 1 casualty on the whole journey, though a few men had colds as the result of it, probably mainly due to the hut deck state in the ship RST	
"	Sun: Ap 25		Spent the day settling in — one troop was moved out to a barn 200 yds from the farm — remainder sleeping in a large barn at	

WAR DIARY
or
INTELLIGENCE SUMMARY.
(Erase heading not required.)

Army Form C. 2118.

P. 3.

Place	Date	Hour	Summary of Events and Information	Remarks and references to Appendices
MEPPE	Ap 25		The farm. Horses were scattered by troops along fences, fastened to trees, high built up ropes. Water quite unsuitable for drinking and difficult in boiling enough for the men. MAJ GEN H.F.C. HEATH CB Cmdg 1/1st SOUTH MIDLAND DIVn visited the Sqdn. RD	
"	Ap 26		O.C. Sqdn saw Lt GEN Sir W.P. PULTENEY KCB DSO Cmdg IIIrd Corps. Horses exercised in morning — dismounted training in reserve trenches in afternoon — signallers and nekometer class resumed practice. RD	
"	Ap 27		Exercised horses in morning — dismtd training in trenches PM	
"	Ap 28		Exercise. Improved billets etc — Washing facilities bad — greatly improved today by digging out a land drainage trench 6ft from a dyke skirting the horse lines — water drawing through	

WAR DIARY
or
INTELLIGENCE SUMMARY.
(Erase heading not required.)

Army Form C. 2118.

P4

Place	Date	Hour	Summary of Events and Information	Remarks and references to Appendices
			6pm of clay silt fault because much cleaner. Water then drawn from tank in knee buckets and men washed in large tubs.	
			[sketch: DYKE — BANK <1'6'> — MUD — TANK 5' — BRICKS]	
			Latrines — 3' deep, 10" wide	
				This has answered well. RSD
NIEPPE	29 Feb		The squadron was ordered to dig trenches in 2nd line during the night and accordingly paraded 6pm and marched to T.17.B.6. Map 1/10000 where horses were tethered along fences - sqdn proceeded on foot to a point 200 yds NW of LA PLUS DOUVE FM and dug communication and fire trenches & drains under direction of R.E. Work lasted 8.30pm — 12.15 am (3AC).	NSD

Army Form C. 2118.

WAR DIARY
or
INTELLIGENCE SUMMARY.
(Erase heading not required.)

P5

Instructions regarding War Diaries and Intelligence Summaries are contained in F.S. Regs., Part II and the Staff Manual respectively. Title pages will be prepared in manuscript.

Place	Date	Hour	Summary of Events and Information	Remarks and references to Appendices
NIEPPE	Ap 29 cont?		Strength of party 100 men Tools — picks 20 — shovels 70 Men were subjected to a certain number of dropping shots but no one was hit. This was the first time they had been under fire of any sort — They paid no attention to it — RDF.	
"	Ap 30		Similar work with same strength was again carried out. This time trees were fastened to a trestle high rope between trees at M.N. corner of PLOEGSTEERT WD. T.16.B.2.8. and men were employed in constructing a redoubt 50 yds N of junction of road from LA PLUS DOUVE FM with WULVERGHEM — MESSINES RD (Trench Map BELGIUM & FRANCE, sheet 28.) — Again a certain amount of sniping fire which seemed to come from close range — 1 man wounded (slight). RDF.	
"	May 1		Times & strength of party as for yesterday's time. Weather, moonlight. No casualties, night dark & wet, men pretty handy. RAD Cont d work, same strength & place.	

Army Form C. 2118.

WAR DIARY
or
INTELLIGENCE SUMMARY.
(Erase heading not required.)

Instructions regarding War Diaries and Intelligence Summaries are contained in F. S. Regs., Part II and the Staff Manual respectively. Title pages will be prepared in manuscript.

P.C.

Place	Date	Hour	Summary of Events and Information	Remarks and references to Appendices
NIEPPE	Sun May 2		Church parade taken by B.P. of PRETORIA. — 30 men under Lt COOPER continued work on redoubt — 6 men wounded. RJT	
"	May 3		The following road reconnaissances were carried out by ptls f Div. HQRS.— ref Sheet 28. (1) CHAPELLE de N.d. GRACE — LE ROSSIGNOL — T10a on ROUTE de MESSINES — NEUVE EGLISE — BAILLEUL ; (2) V.19.B — CALAIS CABARET — NEUVE EGLISE — (3) PLOEGSTEERT — ROMARIN — PAPOT — Remainder 130 men again employed on redoubt. RJT	
"	May 4		Road reconnaissance cont. on all side roads between BAILLEUL — S.#.18.C. — NEUVE-EGLISE — T.10 a. — T.15 A on N. — † BAILLEUL — PONT D'ACHELLES — PAPOT — ROMARIN — PLOEGSTEERT on S. Reports from these two days were satisfactory. Entrenching cont. at night. 1 man wounded. RJT	
"	May 5		Rested — all men had hot bath at PONT de NIEPPE	

Army Form C. 2118.

WAR DIARY
or
INTELLIGENCE SUMMARY.
(Erase heading not required.)

P7

Instructions regarding War Diaries and Intelligence Summaries are contained in F. S. Regs., Part II. and the Staff Manual respectively. Title pages will be prepared in manuscript.

Place	Date	Hour	Summary of Events and Information	Remarks and references to Appendices
DIEPPE	May 6		Roads between PLOEGSTEERT and BOIS de PLOEGSTEERT reported on. Entrenching cont'd (100 men) 1 man badly wounded. 250	
"	May 7		Entrenching cont'd no casualties.	
"	May 8		Entrenching cancelled – exercises 150	
"	Sun May 9		Church parade. Exercise.	
"	May 10		Entrenching continued party 40 men 150 — Saunby inventing + building headwork– O.C. & 2nd designed a bottle carrier for carrying liquid to anti-gas respirators — consisting of wine bottle in ordinary straw cover carried in frame work 7 was forwarded to shops + belts 150	

Army Form C. 2118.

WAR DIARY
or
INTELLIGENCE SUMMARY.
(Erase heading not required.)

P. 8

Place	Date	Hour	Summary of Events and Information	Remarks and references to Appendices
NIEPPE	May 11th		Entrenching continued — 1 sergeant wounded. RSD	
"	May 12th		Entrenching continued RSD	
"	May 13th		" Lieut H.M.H. Cooper wounded — RSD	
"	May 14th		Exercised horses. Signalling & telemeter class revised work RSD	
"	Sun May 15th		Church parade — Exercise — sword & bayonet exercises RSD	
"	May 16		Exercise — Sword & Bayonet drill RSD	
"	May 17		Entrenching having finished the Squadron was put on afresh routine from this day — to include 2 hrs mounted training ; patrol duties, road, river bridge reports etc & 2½ hours dismounted training & lectures including ½ hour each of sword exercise & bayonet exercise. RSD	

1577 Wt.W10791/1773 500,000 1/15 D.D.&L. A.D.S.S./Forms/C. 2118.

Army Form C. 2118.

WAR DIARY
or
INTELLIGENCE SUMMARY.
(Erase heading not required.)

Instructions regarding War Diaries and Intelligence Summaries are contained in F. S. Regs., Part II. and the Staff Manual respectively. Title pages will be prepared in manuscript.

Place	Date	Hour	Summary of Events and Information	Remarks and references to Appendices
NIEPPE	May 18		as for Yesterday	
"	May 19		"	
"	" 20		"	
"	May 21		"	
"	22		"	
"	23		Church parade voluntary	
"	24		as for May 22	
"	25		"	
"	26		musketry practice drill	
"	27		"	
"	28		"	
"	29		"	
"	30		Church parade & as for May 22	
"	May 31		as for May 29th	
"	June 1		"	
"	"		Lecture on infection of small pox	

1577 Wt.W10791/1773 500,000 1/15 D. D. & L. A.D.S.S./Forms/C. 2118.

Army Form C. 2118.

WAR DIARY
or
INTELLIGENCE SUMMARY.
(Erase heading not required.)

Place	Date	Hour	Summary of Events and Information	Remarks and references to Appendices
MEPPE	June 2nd		Instructions dated June 1st from Div. HQRS were received ordering that officers were to be detailed to reconnoitre thoroughly the various lines of defences, strong points, communication trenches and other means of approach by day & night in the divisional area. One officer was therefore detailed to make himself thoroughly acquainted with each Infantry Bde area and work was again begun by the remainder of the Squadron carried on training a division previous to last June. RSP	
		as for June 2nd		RSP
	3rd		"	RSP
	4th		"	RSP
	5th		Check "patrols", reconnoissance by officers and instructions received placing Div. CYCLIST Co. under orders of O.C. Squadron for tactical purposes.	
	6th		Authority 9x363 9 June 6E.	RSP

1577 Wt. W10791/1773 500,000 1/15 D. D. & L. A.D.S.S./Forms/C. 2118.

Army Form C. 2118.

WAR DIARY
or
INTELLIGENCE SUMMARY.
(Erase heading not required.)

Instructions regarding War Diaries and Intelligence Summaries are contained in F. S. Regs., Part II. and the Staff Manual respectively. Title pages will be prepared in manuscript.

Place	Date	Hour	Summary of Events and Information	Remarks and references to Appendices
NEPPE	June 7		The squadron and cyclists were inspected by Maj Gen R. FANSHAWE comdg 48th Div. R.S.	
	June 8		Combined training with the cyclist company during morning parades 8-11 am has begun. R.S.	
	June 9		2 to 4 pm for P.T owing to hot weather - routine was altered. The new time table is :- Reveille 4.30 am., Stables 5-6 am., Troop parade mounted or dismounted 7.15 am. Mounted Parade 8 - 11 am, Stables 11-12. ; Troop parade 4.15 - 5 pm Stables 5-6 pm ; guard mounting 8 pm. R.S.	
	June 10		as for June 9. R.S.	
	11		" R.S.	
	12 Sun		" R.S.	
	13		Church parade ? Exercise R.S.	
	14		as for June 9 R.S.	
	15		" R.S.	
	16		as for June 9 R.S.	

Army Form C. 2118.

WAR DIARY
or
INTELLIGENCE SUMMARY.
(Erase heading not required.)

Instructions regarding War Diaries and Intelligence Summaries are contained in F. S. Regs., Part II. and the Staff Manual respectively. Title pages will be prepared in manuscript.

Place	Date	Hour	Summary of Events and Information	Remarks and references to Appendices
NIEPPE	July		[illegible] and 2nd Lt. [illegible]	
	"18		2nd Lt. F. J. ROMANES joined the squadron from England and was put in command of 3rd Troop. RST	
	"19		Squadron training without cyclists. RAT	
	Sun. 20		Church parade. A draft of 2 shoeing smiths & 10 troopers arrived from England. RST	
	21st		Training with and cyclists. A practice alarm was sounded not at night. The alarm was given at midnight & the squadron men and cyclists Co. moved out to N.W. corner of PLOEGSTEERT WD when drawn near LITT & proceeded to man a section of the subsidiary line S.F. 60 Plus SOUCE F.M. This form having handed Alarm post till the time when the trenches were fully manned. 1hr 35 mins - part of this hinch time was very inferior and corps observed the view moved of outport.	
	22nd		A working party of 2 officers & 16 men into working party from	

WAR DIARY
or
INTELLIGENCE SUMMARY.
(Erase heading not required.)

Army Form C. 2118.

Place	Date	Hour	Summary of Events and Information	Remarks and references to Appendices
MEPPE	Jan 23rd	9 pm – 11.30 pm	Cyclist L.C.P. sent up to improve trenches recently [taken?] from [enemy?]. Standing patrols were sent out to watch for signs of enemy movement in enemy's line. (A) to shelter CHATEAU LA HUTTE, (B) to pt no 2 line in T1873, (C) to pt near DETPIERRE FM. Patrols out — J patrols in position from 7.30 – 9 pm, 2nd set from 2.30 am to 5 am. Each patrol under one NCO with officer i/c line.	RSJ
	23rd		Patrols as for 22nd with exception of all Lewis — signalmen — others to stand by to be ready, however out not to be within ½ hr notice for next 3 days & nights	NSJ
	24th		A. for 23rd. BtB, working parties sent to Same trench as in 23rd James Wise. NCO & 30 men.	NSJ
	25th		A. for 23rd	
	26th		Exercise – preparation for move NSJ	

WAR DIARY
or
INTELLIGENCE SUMMARY.

Army Form C. 2118.

Place	Date	Hour	Summary of Events and Information	Remarks and references to Appendices
VIEUX BERGUIN	June 27	5.30 am	Squadron marched at 5.30 am to starting point 1/2 m NW of NIEPPE on NIEPPE – BAILLEUL RD., Rvce with 'B' Group to VIEUX BERGUIN	
		10.25 am	arrived 10.25 am. Halted till 7.45 pm ten miles.	
		7.45 pm	marched via MERVILLE and ST VENANT to BUSNES, arrived at Khr miles. REST	
		midnight	3/4 m SW of BUSNES at midnight 27th – 28th June. Horses stood march well – no injuries. REST	
BUSNES	June 28		moved to CHATEAU de BUSNES. 1/2 m – bivouaced in park. REST	
BURBURE	June 29	11 am	moved via LILLERS to bivouac on BURBURE – HURIONVILLE RD just NW of BURBURE – Water supply for horses poor. REST	
	June 30		Exercise & Musf ketry – reveille 4.30 am troop parade 7 am REST	

Army Form C. 2118.

WAR DIARY
or
INTELLIGENCE SUMMARY.
(Erase heading not required.)

Place	Date	Hour	Summary of Events and Information	Remarks and references to Appendices
VIEUX BERGUIN	June 27	5:30am	Squadron marched at 5:30 am to starting point to N x W of NIEPPE A NIEPPE — BAILLEUL RD., thence via "B" Group to VIEUX BERGUIN	
		10.25am	arrived 10.25am. Halted NR 7.45pm 16m miles.	
			marched via MERVILLE and ST VENANT to BUSNES, arrived at Killer miles.	
		midnight	½ m SW of BUSNES at midnight 27th – 28th June. Horses stood march well – no injuries.	
BUSNES	June 28		Moved to CHATEAU de BUSNES 12m – bivouacked in park	
BURBURE	June 29	noon	Moved via LILLERS to bivouac in BURBURE – HURIONVILLE RD from Nth of BURBURE – Water supply to horses proven 207	
	June 30		Exercise bareback riding – reveille 4:30 am troop parade 7 am RSM	

WAR DIARY
or
INTELLIGENCE SUMMARY.
(Erase heading not required.)

Army Form C. 2118.

Place	Date	Hour	Summary of Events and Information	Remarks and references to Appendices
BURBURE	July 1		Reveille 4.15 am, other routine as for June 30.	RST
	July 2		as for July 1st. General Sir Douglas Haig KGB etc etc inspected the camp site. Maj Gen Fanshawe Cmdg. 48th Div. RWP into	
	July 3		The following changes in routine took place — 9 Point parades — 5 – 5.30 running & physical exercise — 5.30 – 6.30 stables — 6.30 breakfast rain no parades. All Div. MT Troops Signallers paraded for stables work in the field	
	Sun 4.5		Church parade and exercise.	RST
	5.5		Officers patrols sent out to reconnoitre routes to forward division areas.	RSD
	6.5		M.T. Troops Signallers out for July 3rd	RST
	7.5		Training under troop arrangements	RSD
	8.5		as for July 6	RST

Army Form C. 2118.

WAR DIARY
or
INTELLIGENCE SUMMARY.
(Erase heading not required.)

Place	Date	Hour	Summary of Events and Information	Remarks and references to Appendices
BURBURE	July 9		The squadron took part in a field exercise with the 143rd Inf. Bgd. RSO	
	10		As to July 6.F. — scheme done by squadron. RSO	
	11		Church parade & service. RSO	
	12		Stood by for move. RSO	
	13		ditto RSO	
	14		ditto — more casualties in afternoon. RSO	
	15-16		Scheme for N.C.O's. RSO	
	16		ditto RSO	
	17		Troop training. RSO	
	18		RSO	
	19		The squadron entrained at LA BERGUETTE leaving 4.11 p.m. and travelled in S.P.R. to DOULLENS where it detrained at 9 p.m. and marched to Givenchy at THIÈVRES. Sqn. having been transferred to VII Corps of 3rd Army as from 18th July. Bivouac previously occupied by French troops in very insanitary condition. RSO	
THIÈVRES	25		evacuated the RSO	

Army Form C. 2118.

WAR DIARY
or
INTELLIGENCE SUMMARY.
(Erase heading not required.)

Instructions regarding War Diaries and Intelligence Summaries are contained in F. S. Regs., Part II. and the Staff Manual respectively. Title pages will be prepared in manscript.

Place	Date	Hour	Summary of Events and Information	Remarks and references to Appendices
THIEVRES	July 21		Morphrining Exercises Sept 187.	
AUTHIE	22nd		Squadron moved between [?] at AUTHIE (2m) & have been in lying of my horses.	
"	25th		Morphraining 187	
"	Sp [?]		" 187	
"	Sun 25th		Church parade service 187 auto 24th	
"	26		187	
"	27		2 foot domain path under an officer are asked to be found by the squadron and equalist company attempts from the late. These paths were in [?] to support Hucken pit N6 and SE of HEBUTERNE respectively until ordered to be on duty from 1 hour before dawn until dusk. — Remainder [?] of day morphraining &c 187	
			187	
	30		187	
	31		Sqdr moved between at Bks LES ARTONS. Horses have to be sent 2½ miles to water. EST	

48th Division

121/6901

B. Squad'n King Edwards Horse
(48th Div¹. Cavalry)

Vol II

Aug & Sept. 15

"Confidential"

War Diary

of

'B' Squadron, King Edward's Horse.

From 1.8.15   To 30.IX.15

(Volume I.)

WAR DIARY or INTELLIGENCE SUMMARY

Army Form C. 2118.

Place	Date	Hour	Summary of Events and Information	Remarks and references to Appendices
BUS LES ARTIS	Aug 1st		Exercise and ck RST	
	2nd		Exercise Troop training RST	
	3rd		"	
	4th		" — A working party of 1 Off & 73 men found to improving road beside NE of SAILLY AUX BOIS, digging drains — repairing parapets etc. RST	
	5th		Working party as for yesterday. Observation post. — RST	
	6th		no 5th sunf. RST	
	7th		ditto Rst	
	8th		ditto RST	
	9th		Working party — observation posts taken over by cyclists. Lt A.F. CRESWICK reported for duty from 'A' Sqdn. Also posted to 1st Troop. Lt Troop via Capt A SCHWANN from B.S.	
	10th		General troop training 2 RMP found from today. It was arranged that MO should inspect smoke helmets & respirators every Thurs & Sunday. RST	
	11th		Working party	
	12th		Working party of 4 NCO's & men per troop	

Army Form C. 2118.

WAR DIARY
or
INTELLIGENCE SUMMARY.
(Erase heading not required.)

Place	Date	Hour	Summary of Events and Information	Remarks and references to Appendices
BUS LES ARTOIS	Aug 13.		Entrenching continued on same sector. RST	
	14		ditto	
			fire trenches. NE and SE of HEBUTERNE. 2 Observation posts found behind our RST	
	15		ditto	
	16		" " " 2/Lt. RSD RST	
	17		" " RST	
	18		" " ½RST	
	19		No trenching men sent to baths; both relieved by cyclist company for 5 days. RST	
			entrenching continued RST	
	19		" " RST	
	20		" " RST	
	21		" " RST	
	22ⁿᵈ		horses grazed - voluntary church parade RST	
	23ʳᵈ		as for 2 RST - wire party working hurdles to stocking RST	
	24ᵗʰ		entrenching - observation posts. RST	

Army Form C. 2118.

WAR DIARY
or
INTELLIGENCE SUMMARY.
(Erase heading not required.)

Place	Date	Hour	Summary of Events and Information	Remarks and references to Appendices.
LBVC	25th		Entrenching – observation posts RDF	
LES ARTOIS	26th		ditto	
	27th		Entrenching CSF	
	28th		Entrenching CRSF	
	29th		Church parade & troop training RSF	
	30th		Battalion parade by half squadrons RSF	
	31st		Entrenching RSF	
			Troop training RSF	
Sept 1915			Troop training RSF	
	2nd			
	3rd		Work begun on constructing new covered stables for the winter RSF	
	4th		Building stables & clearing out & repairing visible billets RSD	
	5th		Church parade – working party to do new movements RSF	
	6th		Work on stables and billets RSF	
	7th		Tactical schemes with squadron RSF	
	8th		Work on stables & rebuilding billets RSF	
	9th		ditto ... battalion parade & sqdn RSF	

WAR DIARY
or
INTELLIGENCE SUMMARY.

Army Form C. 2118.

Place	Date	Hour	Summary of Events and Information	Remarks and references to Appendices
BUS les ARTOIS	Sept 10	—	Work on stables and billets, positioning — skeleton tactical scheme (advanced guard) units visited — cyclist C? RST	
	11th	—	Yesterday's scheme repeated RST	
	12th	—	Church parade. Inspection problem etc. RST	
	13th	—	Entrenching ... RST	
	14th	—	Entrenching, combined — "Northern rifles" ON W? Fo? QUEVILLERS reconnoitred by officers patrol. Sqdr orders to be redistributed at ½ hours notice. RST	
	15th	—	Entrenching RST	
	16th	—	Entrenching RST	
	17th	—	... RST	
	18th	—	... RST	
	19th	—	Worked day, church parade in afternoon RST	
	20th	—	Tactical exercise (advance) — ? party with cyclist C?, ₤ Draft of 11 men joined the squadron :- RST	
	22nd	—	Entrenching — 4 snipers daily to be detailed for 24 hours duty in the trenches beginning today. RST	

WAR DIARY or INTELLIGENCE SUMMARY

Army Form C. 2118.

p 22

Place	Date	Hour	Summary of Events and Information	Remarks and references to Appendices
BVS les ARTOIS	Sept 22nd	—	Entrenching continued. RST.	
	23rd	—	No working parties at work on billets and general inspection of equipment made. RST	
	24th	—	Squadron drills in afternoon RST	
	25th	—	Gazing parade in morning, squadron drill afternoon	
	26th	—	Grazing (3rd Troop and 'B' RAINCHEVAL as Corps mounted troops). Corps. RST Battery of horse & foot artillery in squadron lines RST	
	26th	—	Grazing, bathing and Squadron drill. RST	
	27th	—	as for 26th. 7 remounts received. RST	
	28th	—	as for 27th. RST	
	29th	—	Grazing and foot parade. RST	
	30th	—	Inspection of horses in camp by ADVS 4th Div. Troop training in afternoon. During the month 15 horses have been trained as bombers. RST	

12/7333

46th Batt"

B. Squadron King Edward's Horse
(48th Dist. Corp.)

Vol III.

Oct 15

Confidential

War Diary
of
"B" Squadron, King Edward's Horse. (K.O.D.R.)

(Volume 1)

From 1st Octr. 1915.   to 31st Octr. 1915.

Initialled by the Officer keeping Diary (Capt. R.S. Hume)

M. S. Steele
Major
Comdg "B" Sqn K.E.H.

Army Form C. 2118.

P 23

WAR DIARY
or
INTELLIGENCE SUMMARY.
(Erase heading not required.)

Instructions regarding War Diaries and Intelligence Summaries are contained in F. S. Regs., Part II. and the Staff Manual respectively. Title pages will be prepared in manuscript.

Place	Date	Hour	Summary of Events and Information	Remarks and references to Appendices
BVS	Oct 1st	-	Squadron detailed trenching on Fridays Saturdays in each week. 7 hours work per day.	
	2nd Sun 3rd	-	Entrenching continued. RST	
		-	Entrenching. RST	
		-	Church parade. Reveillí put to 5am. RST	
	4th	-	Tactical exercise in morning – cleaning and inspection of saddlery in afternoon. All wagons employed drawing chalk to floor of winter stables. RST	
	5th	-	Tactical exercise in morning – work on stables in afternoon. RST	
	6th	-	A 200 yd rifle range having been fixed up near the billets a short musketry practice was fired by troops leaving today. Remainder working on stables. Fresh bombing class of 8 men per troop was formed. RST	
	7th	-	Musketry and work on stables. RST	
		-	7 men gas started. RST	
	8th	-	Musketry – work on stables. RST	
	9th	-	A class of men chosen that lastly orders was turned for daily musketry instruction – remainder building stables. RST	

Army Form C. 2118.

WAR DIARY
or
INTELLIGENCE SUMMARY.
(Erase heading not required.)

p. 24

Place	Date	Hour	Summary of Events and Information	Remarks and references to Appendices
BUS	Oct 10th	—	Church parade — work on stables during morning. Battling by troops RSF	
	11th	—	Battling by troops, musketry, class, work on stables. RSF	
	12th	—	As for 11th RSF	
	13th	—	Work on stables — farrier RSF	
	14th	—	Work on stables, musketry. RSF	
	15th	—	Work on stables — From today, horses watered twice daily 10am & 4pm	
			Instead of 3 times, musketry. RSF	
	16th	—	Work on stables — musketry class. RSF	
	17th	—	Work on stables in the morning. Church parade. Kit inspection RSF	
	18th	—	Work on stables, musketry, battling, 1 troop. RSF	
	19th	—	Work on stables — musketry. RSF	
	20th	—	As for 19th. An NCO was accidentally killed by a talk of chalk when working in a chalk pit. RSF	
	21st	—	As for 18th. RSF Stables	
	22nd	—	Horses grazed — walks on stables, billets Swadroom. RSF	
	23rd	—	As for 22nd. RSF etc.	

Army Form C. 2118.

WAR DIARY
or
INTELLIGENCE SUMMARY.
(Erase heading not required.)

Instructions regarding War Diaries and Intelligence Summaries are contained in F. S. Regs., Part II. and the Staff Manual respectively. Title pages will be prepared in manuscript.

Place	Date	Hour	Summary of Events and Information	Remarks and references to Appendices
BUS LES ARTOIS	Sun. Oct 24	—	Church parade, saddlery and kit inspection. RST.	
	" 25	—	Work, musketry - grazing - musketry. RST.	
	" 26	—	As for 25th. RST.	
	" 27	—	As for 25th. Pony in afternoon. RST.	
	" 28	—	As for 25th. RST.	
	" 29	—	As for 25th. RST.	
	" 30	—	Work, musketry, grazing, musketry - saddlery inspection. RST.	
	Sun 31st	—	Church parade - grazing in morning.	
			During the month the Squadron has continued to find the Horse Observation posts near HEBUTERNE. The Cyclists Company & Observation has been continuous from daylight till dark every day. RST	

1577 Wt.W10791/1773 500,000 1/15 D.D.&L. A.D.S.S./Forms/C. 2118.

48th K.U. own.

Confidential.

War Diary
of
B. Squadron, King Edward's Horse.

From 1st Nov. 1915 to 30th Nov. 1915

IV
(Volume)

Army Form C. 2118.

WAR DIARY
or
INTELLIGENCE SUMMARY.
(Erase heading not required.)

P 76

Place	Date	Hour	Summary of Events and Information	Remarks and references to Appendices
BUS	Nov 2nd		Work returns, canteen, ablution sheds etc. R.S.F.	
	Nov 3rd		as for yesterday. R.S.F.	
	3rd		ditto - R.S.F.	
	4th		ditto - R.S.F.	
	5th		ditto - R.S.F.	
	6th		ditto - R.S.F.	
	7th		Work as usual in morning. Voluntary church parade. R.S.F.	
	8th		Full marching order parade for inspection. Squadron drill — work on stables in afternoon. R.S.F.	
	9th		Work ablution stables etc. R.S.F.	
	10th		Work on billets — pay parade. R.S.F.	
	11th		Work ablutions etc. R.S.F.	
	12th		The horses were put into stables today and seemed do much better. The mud outside lines has been very bad indeed for some time and there has been a lot of cold & wet weather. Considering the conditions they have stood it well. There have only been six men on sick lines on an average. R.S.F.	

Army Form C. 2118.

WAR DIARY
or
INTELLIGENCE SUMMARY.
(Erase heading not required.)

P27

Place	Date	Hour	Summary of Events and Information	Remarks and references to Appendices
BUS	Nov 13th	—	Woke in billets etc. There was a heavy gale and rain last night but the stables have it stood it very well. It had been feared the roofs might go in a very heavy wind. RST	
	14th Sun	—	Woke in billets. Cleared midday - church parade. Heavy gale again: in stables all right. DD	
	15th	—	Woke in billets etc RST	
	16th	—	A pretty heavy fall of snow last night, but to white roof stood its weight. This and the wind more had been more feared. Woke in billets — RST	
	17th	—	Woke in billets etc. very cold and a little more snow. RST	
	18th	—	Work as usual in billets and staff observation posts between SAILLY & COXIN CAMPS. Canteen opened comprising dry canteen, beer, & reading room. RST	
	19th	—	Work as usual in billets & observation posts. RST	
	20th	—	ditto RST	
	21st	—	Saddle cleaning etc. in Church parade. The horses are thinning	

Army Form C. 2118.

WAR DIARY
or
INTELLIGENCE SUMMARY.
(Erase heading not required.)

P 28

Place	Date	Hour	Summary of Events and Information	Remarks and references to Appendices
BVS	Nov 21st cont	—	Definite improvement already in appearance since they have gone under canv. The canteen appears to be a considerable success. R.S.F.	
	22nd	—	Work as usual on billets & ablution sheds & observation posts. R.S.F.	
	23rd	—	Fatigue work as usual. 2 A.R. recruits received, increasing the strength. R.S.F.	
	24/F	—	Fatigue work — boy. R.S.F.	
	25/F	—	A scheme of recruits training was begun on the following lines — musketry class to tent pitchers & hygiene. Troop parade mounted 8 – 9.30am; dismounted for sword & bayonet exercise and physical drill 1.45 – 2.30 pm — R.S.F.	
	26/F	—	act as yesterday. Training greatly hampered by the numbers now away on fatigue and detached duty and also by the length of time taken to get to & from the watering place, which is over 2½ miles from the lines. Observation posts taken on by 4 days. R.S.F.	
	27/F	—	Church parade — hot mis-hetoris praying. R.S.F.	

WAR DIARY or INTELLIGENCE SUMMARY

Army Form C. 2118.

P29

Place	Date	Hour	Summary of Events and Information	Remarks and references to Appendices
BUS LES ARTOIS	Nov 28th	—	Weather Saturday 28th... A reinforcement of 15 men [?] showing smart and spirited [?] was taken on this strength. RST.	
	29 F	—	Work as for yesterday. My heavy rain. RST.	
	30 S	—	Work on manual rifle. An experiment in using grenades mounted has carried out, in this manner. The target was a trame work of poles leaving an aperture 3' high and 6' wide to represent the rear opening of a gun emplacement. This was placed with the edge of a steep drop an approximate Smile [?] were thrown at the Sadly [?] by the heading [?] trying to Capt Turner and Sergt Watson's. All of the shots were successful and there were plenty of rifle grenades thrown over adrop and of range 7. [?] ... RST.	
			[illegible lines]... that he believes [illegible] ...	

Confidential

War Diary
of

B Squadron King Edward's Horse. K.O.D.R.

from

December 1st to 31st 1915

Vol V

Army Form C. 2118.

WAR DIARY
or
INTELLIGENCE SUMMARY.
(Erase heading not required.)

Instructions regarding War Diaries and Intelligence Summaries are contained in F. S. Regs., Part II. and the Staff Manual respectively. Title pages will be prepared in manuscript.

Place	Date	Hour	Summary of Events and Information	Remarks and references to Appendices
BUS LES ARTOIS	Dec 1st		Troop parade 8 – 9.30 a.m. Road making fatigue 13 men to COIGNEUX. Musketry class 1st officers & sergeants 1.45 – 2.45 pm & 6.30 – 7.30 pm	
	2nd		Dismounted agondum training 1.45 – 2.30 pm. RST	
	3rd		as for yesterday – bathing by troops. RST	
	4th		" " RST	
	5th		RST	
	6th		Church parade – clothing inspection RST	
	7th		as for 4th inst RST	
	8th		as for yesterday RST	
	9th		RST	
	10th		RST	
	11th		RST	
	Sun 12th		" " RST	
	13th		Church parade RST	
	14th		as for last inst RST	
			" " RST	

WAR DIARY
or
INTELLIGENCE SUMMARY.

Army Form C. 2118.

P31

Place	Date	Hour	Summary of Events and Information	Remarks and references to Appendices
BUS LES ARTOIS	Dec 15th		as for 14th inst. RST	
	16th		" " RST	
	17th		" " RST	
	18th		" " RST	
	19th		Church parade. RST	
	20th		up to 18:45 – bathing by troops at the new showery baths in BUS. RST	
	21st		" " " " " RST	
	22nd		work on huts etc hay – RST	
	23rd		work as usual RST	
	24th Xmas Day		" " RST	
	25th		church parade – holiday – RST	
	26th		entries as for last week. Special instruction in use of tube helmets given daily from to-day. RST	
			routine as usual RST	
	27th		" " horses & mules	
	28th		" for Gladdon by Mallin Ker RST	
	29th		work is as usual RST	

Army Form C. 2118.

WAR DIARY
or
INTELLIGENCE SUMMARY.
(Erase heading not required.)

P 3 a

Place	Date	Hour	Summary of Events and Information	Remarks and references to Appendices
BnS 1ST s ARTISTS	Dec 30		Routine as usual	
	31		"	

1577 Wt.W10791/1773 500,000 1/15 D. D. & L.   A.D.S.S./Forms/C. 2118.

Confidential

WAR DIARY OF
'B' SQUADRON   KING EDWARDS HORSE [K.O.R.]

VOL XVI

From Jan 1st — 31st 1916

A. J. Dick
Major
Commanding 'B' Squadron
King Edwards Horse

WAR DIARY
INTELLIGENCE SUMMARY

B. Sqdn
KING EDWARD HORSE
K.E.H.R.

Place	Date	Hour	Summary of Events and Information	Remarks and references to Appendices
BUS LES ARTOIS	1916 Jan 1st		Routine as usual — tube helmet practice — saddlery + transport cleaned — RST.	P 33 [Vi x P1]
	2nd		Church parade — a start was made in giving wagon 24 hr training in the trenches — 8 n.c.o's and men in each party — Trench Mortar sections 14.15 and 16, E 28.c.1.7.6 E 27.d 81.35 held in rotation by 1/7th and 1/8th R Warwicks of 143rd Inf. Bde:— These detours are being continually harassed by minenwerfer from GOMME COURT wood. — RST	
	3rd		Routine as usual RST.	
	4th		" " " RST.	
	5th		" " " RST	
	6th		" " - batting RST	
	7th		" " " RST	
	8th		" " " RST.	
	9th		Church parade RST.	

WAR DIARY
or
INTELLIGENCE SUMMARY.

Army Form C. 2118.

Place	Date	Hour	Summary of Events and Information	Remarks and references to Appendices
BUSNES	Jan 10th		The Squadron was visited by the Commander in Chief. R.S.T.	
	11th		Routine as usual. R.S.T.	
	12th		Carried on batting. R.S.T.	
	13th		[illegible] R.S.T.	
	14th		[illegible] R.S.T.	
	15th		[illegible] R.S.T.	
	16th		Church Parade. R.S.T.	
	17th		All officers having been detailed, proceeded with Capt. Sephen with Cyclist Co. find a party of 1 officer and 30 men daily for the trenches as mentioned above. They are responsible for the front line entirely by day and in company with a platoon of the Bn in the line by night — they are under orders of the Company holding that section — Each party does 24 hrs. R.S.T.	
	18th		As for yesterday — batting. 1 Sergt & 13 privates arrived as reinforcement from the base and were taken on strength. R.S.T.	
	19th		Routine as for yesterday — hay. balling. R.S.T. 1 horse died pneumonia. R.S.T.	

WAR DIARY
or
INTELLIGENCE SUMMARY.

(Erase heading not required.)

Army Form C. 2118.

P35. (V61 x P 3)

Place	Date	Hour	Summary of Events and Information	Remarks and references to Appendices
BUS LES ARTOIS	Jan 20th		Routine as usual – LI. RSF.	
	21st		Routine as usual – RSF.	
	22nd		" Divisional taken on through	
	23rd		baths. Church Parade RSF.	
	24th		Routine as usual – bathing RSF.	
	25th	2am	About 2am our trenches commanded by LIEUT W.D. BELL were heavily bombarded with HE, canister bombs – m.g. & rifle fire. While the sections in trenches were raided by an enemy party of No. ? casualties to R.E.H. men.	
		3.15am	Alarm received suddenly & party who turned out at 3.15am & hit were withdrawn ? RSF ?	
	26th		Routine as usual RSF & ?	
	27th		At ? a.m. notifying preparation ready for action to march ? detailed for the future to suffer work with ? a gas alarm received at 7.50 pm – orders to turn out & proceed to 3pm ? Sgt turned out in fighting order with sea timber & pack and 1 male –	

Army Form C. 2118.

WAR DIARY
or
INTELLIGENCE SUMMARY.
(Erase heading not required.)

Instructions regarding War Diaries and Intelligence Summaries are contained in F. S. Regs, Part II. and the Staff Manual respectively. Title pages will be prepared in manuscript.

Place	Date	Hour	Summary of Events and Information	Remarks and references to Appendices
Bus	Jan 27th		Officers patrol sent to HEBUTERNE and K.21.b.z.8. under Lt Romanes	
			Observation posts manned. Squadron not sent out –	
	28th		Patrols dismissed 12 midnight. 27/28 R57. Routine as usual. R57.	
	29th		Gas reported by 16th Corps to S.E. received 7.30 am – no further steps ordered. R57	
	30th		Kit inspection R57.	
	31st		Routine as usual. R57.	

CONFIDENTIAL

WAR DIARY
of
"B" Squadron
KING EDWARDS HORSE.
K.O.D.R.

From Feb 1st – Feb 29th 1916. Vol VII

VOL IX. p1 to 3.

N. L. Bich Major
Commanding B Sqdn
King Edwards Horse

Army Form C. 2118.

WAR DIARY
or
INTELLIGENCE SUMMARY.

'B' Squadron
KING EDWARDS HORSE
K.O.D.R
P37 [VOL XI P I]

Place	Date	Hour	Summary of Events and Information	Remarks and references to Appendices
BUS LES ARTOIS	Feb 1st		Troop training – Six remounts taken on strength.	
	2nd		taken on strength. 2 privates. 1 trumpeter. 1 shoeing smith. RST. Troop training – batting. 15 details went for instruction in trenches SE of FONQUEVILLERS returning same day. RD	Following rein from
	3rd		Troop training. RST.	
	4th		" " RD	
	5th		" " RSF.	
	6th		Church parade, saddlery inspection. RD	
	7th		Troop training. The squadron association football XI were beaten by 2 goals to 1 in the semi-final of the GOC's cup open to all the division – a poor performance put the smallest men to	
	8th		get return. RST. Troop training RST.	
	9th		" " batting RST.	
	10th		" " RST.	
	11th		" " RSF	

WAR DIARY or INTELLIGENCE SUMMARY.

Army Form C. 2118.

"B" Squadron KING EDWARD'S HORSE
P 38 [vol XI p 2]

Place	Date	Hour	Summary of Events and Information	Remarks and references to Appendices
BUS LES ARTOIS	Aug 12.		Troop training. R&T	
	13.		Church parade. R&T	
	14.		Troop training. R&T	
	15.		Battery - Troop training - all remaining details sent to pits sent in trenches R&T	
	16.		Troop training. R&T	
	17.		" "	
	18.		" " 1 remount taken on draught R&T	
	19.		" " batting R&T	
	20.	7pm	Infy wire piquet turned out for patrol 7pm. only to attack N.12.b. Brigade - Patrol not turn out. R&T	
	21.		Church parade. R&T	
	22.		Troop training, 3 new recruits arrived. R&T	
	23.		Troop training - batting. R&T	
	24.		Troop " R&T	
	25.		Troop training # horse . R&T	
	26.		Show front very cold - Dismounted training - all horses roughed. R&T	
	27.		Dismounted training . R&T	
			Church parade. R&T	

WAR DIARY or INTELLIGENCE SUMMARY.

Army Form C. 2118.

"B" Squadron
KING EDWARDS HORSE
(C.O.2.R)
Pg. E Vol XI p.2)

Place	Date	Hour	Summary of Events and Information	Remarks and references to Appendices
BUS LES ARTOIS	Feb 28th		Troop training	
	29th		Troop training. Resumé of month. The squadron has greatly benefited by being withdrawn from fatigue work and trenches and given an opportunity for training — The horses have improved in condition and the men have greatly improved in smartness & bearing and have come up definitely during the month's training. Up till 25th Feb the Squadron was doing so much outside work that training was practically impossible — trainmen were very short handed & it was hoped that an average of 4 to 5 hours hand to be toleration and after Manœuvring Knee up by hand or sector duty in trenches in every 8 days although all officers & hands & troop sergts were employed on fatigue duty. (2) The Observation posts have continued without interruption. The G.O.C. awarded 2 extra leaves to up land during the month for good Observation work. R.S.L.	

CONFIDENTIAL

WAR DIARY
of

"B" Sqdn   KING EDWARDS. HORSE

from 1st Mch   to 31st Mch 1916

Vol VIII

L. F. Sil.
Major
Comdg "B" Sqs KEH

Army Form C. 2118.

WAR DIARY 'B' Sqdn. KING EDWARDS HORSE
or
INTELLIGENCE SUMMARY. [P 40. Vol XII ...]

(Erase heading not required.)

Instructions regarding War Diaries and Intelligence Summaries are contained in F. S. Regs., Part II. and the Staff Manual respectively. Title pages will be prepared in manuscript.

Place	Date	Hour	Summary of Events and Information	Remarks and references to Appendices
BUS LES	March 1		Troop training - pm RST	
ARTOIS	2		Troop training RST	
	3		" " RST	
	4		" " talking RST	
	5		Church parade. Lieut H.F. Cressick promoted Capt noted 29/1/16 RST	
	6		Troop training RST	
	7		" " RST	
	8		" " RST	
	9		" " Lt Bell and 2 nco's sent for training	
	10		Course in Hotchkiss gun RST	
	11		Troop training RST	
	12		Church parade RST	
	13		Troop training RST	
	14		" " RST	
	15		" " RST 3 other ranks reinforcement arrived RST	

Army Form C. 2118.

ESQUADRON HORSE
K.O.D.R
B. Sqdn KING'S
P.41
[Vol XII p 2]

WAR DIARY
or
INTELLIGENCE SUMMARY.
(Erase heading not required.)

Instructions regarding War Diaries and Intelligence Summaries are contained in F. S. Regs., Part II. and the Staff Manual respectively. Title pages will be prepared in manuscript.

Place	Date	Hour	Summary of Events and Information	Remarks and references to Appendices
BUS LES ARTOIS	Mar 16th		Squadron training tactical exercise for inspection by G.O.C. 48th Div. RSF	
	17th		L⁰ duty. L⁰ Romanes & 30 NCO's & men instructed in traffic control duties by 2. P.m. RSF	
	17:40		" " RSF	
	18:40		Squadron Troop training RSF	
	19th		Troop training RSF	
	20th		Church Parade. Alarm - Sqdn turned out & in readiness RSF	
	21st		Troop training RSF	
	"		" 18 hour's men attached to Military Police for traffic control RSF	
	22nd		Troop training - battalion RSF	
	23rd		" " RSF	
	24th		" " RSF	
	25th		Fatigue work preparatory to move RSF	
COUIN	26th		Headquarters moved into billets at COUIN. RSF	
COUIN	27th		Fatigue Sqn RSF	
"	28th		" " RSF	

Army Form C. 2118.

WAR DIARY
or
INTELLIGENCE SUMMARY.
(Erase heading not required.)

'B' Sqn KING EDWARD'S HORSE KOTIK.

Place	Date	Hour	Summary of Events and Information	Remarks and references to Appendices
COUIN	May 29th		Fatigue. signallers class. RSF.	
	30th		" " RSF	
	31st		" " RSF	
			Notes on Month. (1) Observation. The observation posts have continued and have done some very good work. The G.O.C. allotted 1 extra leave for this — definite improvement in condition. RSF	
			(2) Horses RSF	

48

CONFIDENTIAL

WAR DIARY
of
"B" Sqdn. KING EDWARD'S HORSE
K.O.T.T.
VOL. XIV IX

From April 1st to 30th 1916

3 Jun
1/5/16

M. F. Beck
Major
Cmdg "B" Sqn
KING EDWARD'S HORSE

WAR DIARY
INTELLIGENCE SUMMARY

Army Form C. 2118.

'B' Sqdn KING EDWARDS HORSE
K.O.D.T.
Pa3 Vol XVII PI

Place	Date	Hour	Summary of Events and Information	Remarks and references to Appendices
COUIN	Apr 1		Fatigues - Signallers class - bathing. NST	
	2		Church parade - Clothing inspection RST	
	3		Tactical scheme under direction of G.O.C., the Sqdn aching as vanguard to the Div moving on a front of 3½ mile. NST	
	4		Pte Wheatley Smith JM returned from 3 months duty with MGC. The APM expressed his "full appreciation" of their work. RST	
	5		Musketry training. Signallers class as before. 3rd NST	
	6		Tactical scheme as per app. 3rd NST	
	7		Work as usual NST	
	8		Musketry practice on 200 yd range NST	
	9		— NST	
	10		Church parade - Clothing inspection RST	
	11		Tactical exercise with cyclist Coy. RST	
	12		Preparations for move - The Sqdn being under orders to proceed to 2nd Indian Cavalry Divn for training NST	

Army Form C. 2118.

WAR DIARY
or
INTELLIGENCE SUMMARY.
(Erase heading not required.)

B. Sqdn. KING EDWARD'S HORSE

Vol XIII p 2

Place	Date	Hour	Summary of Events and Information	Remarks and references to Appendices
ST OUEN	12	12:45	The sqdn. with cyclist Coy. marched from LOUIN via BEAUQUESNE and CANAPLES to ST OUEN (ref 1:40,000 AMIENS sheet) where it billetted. RAT	
ACHEUX-EN-VIMEU	13	13:45	March continued via FLIXECOURT and LIMEUXCOURT to ACHEUX-EN-VIMEU where sqdn. came under orders of 2nd Indian Car. Div. — March discipline on the whole very good. Transport marched well in spite of some bad hills. RAT	
		14:15	Very wet. Brigade scheme cancelled. RAT	
		15:15	Tactical Exercise — Major Ditch KEH commanding B Sq. KEH and 2 Sq. 2nd DECCAN HORSE & 2 sqs. 4H & 1 cyclist Coy. RAT	
		16:15	January offday. RAT	
		17:15	Very wet. Scheme cancelled. RAT	
		18:45	Bde. Exercise — occupying & holding position until arrival of infantry. The sqdn. held village of TOEUFFLES. RAT	
ST RIGUIER	20		Sqdn. marched with brigade via ABBEVILLE to ST RIGUIER RAT under Maj. Dyer — 7th D.G. RAT	
	21			
	22		—	RAT
	23		Squadron training scheme under Maj. Dyer	RAT

Army Form C. 2118.

"B" Sqdn KING EDWARD HORSES
N - O - D - Q

P45. vol XIII P3

WAR DIARY
or
INTELLIGENCE SUMMARY.
(Erase heading not required.)

Instructions regarding War Diaries and Intelligence Summaries are contained in F.S. Regs., Part II. and the Staff Manual respectively. Title pages will be prepared in manuscript.

Place	Date	Hour	Summary of Events and Information	Remarks and references to Appendices
ST RIQUIER	Apr 25th		Apr 23rd NSR. Sqdn and cyclist Coy carried out a new found scheme NEI. ONEX v the Secunderabad Brigade. Rot	
			ANNEX	
JOUEN	26th		Marched to ST OUEN (11 miles) - NST	
COUIN	27th		Marched via CAMPLES & REMUGUESNE to COUIN returning 48th Div. Horses picketed out overnight. RST	
	28th		Signatters cleaning. Cleaning up. RSD	
	29th		Signatters class. Dismounted parades - 2nd Lt R.W. HOPE arrived from England and posted to 1st Troop RST	
	30th		Church parade. Capt R.S. FURSE attached temporarily to 9. Brunel - General Staff 4th Div. RSD	
			NOTES. (a) Observation work continues up to 14th inst. (b) March discipline found with Sqdn with exception Car. was satisfactory. The S.O.C. RST expresses himself as very satisfied with work of the Sqdn. Horses considerably improved in condition RST	

Confidential

DUPLICATE

WAR DIARY.
of
"B" Sqdn — KING EDWARDS HORSE

From 1st May 1916 — May 31st 1916.

WAR DIARY or INTELLIGENCE SUMMARY

Army Form C. 2118.

B Sqdn
KING EDWARDS HORSE
K.O.D.R.
p 46 (Vol XIV p.1)

Place	Date	Hour	Summary of Events and Information	Remarks and references to Appendices
COUIN	May 1		Troop parade (moved in morning, dismounted in afternoon) — Signalling class. b/fots	
	2		As for first day b/fots	
	3		As for yesterday b/fots	
	4		As for yesterday b/fots	
	5		As for yesterday b/fots	
	6		As for yesterday b/fots	
	7		Church parade — bathing b/fots	
	8		Horses clipped — one leader for march-dress — b/fots	
ECOIVRES	9		Preparing for move — horses are great — bay mare loaded. b/fots	
	10		Marched via DOUBLENS to ECOIVRES (4 miles N. of FREVENT) (Ry hq LENS!!) £10,000 thro Sqdn billeted — horse picketed out b/fots Sqdn was inspected by the G.O.C. VIII Corps who expressed himself as pleased with the general appearance of Sqdn and conveyed a message from G.O.C. 48th Div.	
	11		from commanding Rehabilitation task-work done by Sqdn whilst with 48th Div. b/fots Marched via ST.POL — OSTREVILLE — DIEVAL — BRUAY to CHOCQUES where	
CHOCQUES	11		Sqdn billeted — horses picketed out — joined I Corps. b/fots	
	12		Horses rest — usual routine b/fots	

Army Form C. 2118.

"B" Sqdn
KING EDWARDS HORSE
K.O.D.R
p. 47 (Vol XII p.2)

WAR DIARY
or
INTELLIGENCE SUMMARY
(Erase heading not required.)

Place	Date	Hour	Summary of Events and Information	Remarks and references to Appendices
MAREST	May 13		Marched via MARLES-LES-MINES to MAREST (2 miles S of PERNES) where Sqdn billeted — horses picketed out — joined IV Corps troops	
	14		Horses rested — visual & audible tests	
	15		Horses exercised and groomed — Capt H.T CHATFIELD RAMC ass formed Sqdn on temporary attachment. Sqdn for all purposes.	
	16		Marched to VALHUON (time Sqdn leaves — horses fed and watered. Sqdn billeted Francis [illegible]	
VALHUON	17		8 N.C.O's [illegible]	
"	18		Hotchkiss gun Course was held here. [illegible]	
"	19		Routine as usual — Hotchkiss [illegible]	
"	20		Horse exercise — Signallers [illegible] [illegible] troops [illegible]	
"	21		Clothing inspection — horse exercise — C of E service [illegible]	
"	22		Routine as usual — horses exercised — Officers above [illegible]	
"	23		Routine as yesterday — 1 N.C.O. and 10 men departed for [illegible] duty with 2nd Divn [illegible]	

2449 Wt. W14957/M90 750,000 1/16 J.B.C. & A. Forms/C.2118/12

WAR DIARY or INTELLIGENCE SUMMARY

Army Form C. 2118.

"B" Sqdn
KING EDWARDS HORSE
p. 48 (Vol XIV F.3)

Place	Date	Hour	Summary of Events and Information	Remarks and references to Appendices
VALHUON	May 24		Routine as yesterday — 11 men despatched for duty with 23rd Divn. Infantry	
	"25		Routine as yesterday. Infantry	
	"26		E. Horses exercised + holding parade. Infantry	
	"27		Routine as usual — 8 N.C.O's returned to duty from IV Corps School of Instruction. Infantry	
	"28		Horses exercised in A.M. E. Ranges P.M. Infantry	
	"29		Routine as usual. Infantry	
	"30		Routine as usual — Fay — Infantry	
	"31		Routine as usual — Lt Rose returned to duty from IV Corps Depot of Instruction. A+C Sqdns King Edwards Horse (KODR) arrived at VALHUON and Major SUTHERMON (C Sqdn) assumed command of the Regiment. 1/4/18.	

From. O.C. "B" Sqdn 1st King Edwards Horse
To   D.A.G. Base.

From 31st May 1916 the War Diary will be kept regimentally

W.J. Dick Major
Commdg B Sqdn. K.E.H

2/6/16